序. 144

BRIGHT IDEA BOOKS

HOW DID Robots LAND ON MARS?

by Clara MacCarald

Content Consultant

Jim Bell
Professor, School of Earth and
Space Exploration
Arizona State University

CAPSTONE PRESS
a capstone imprint

Bright Idea Books are published by Capstone Press
1710 Roe Crest Drive, North Mankato, Minnesota 56003
www.mycapstone.com

Library of Congress Cataloging-in-Publication Data
Library of Congress Cataloging-in-Publication Data is available on the Library of Congress website.
ISBN: 978-1-5435-4136-6 (library hardcover)
ISBN: 978-1-5435-4176-2 (eBook PDF)

Editorial Credits
Editor: Megan Gunderson
Designer: Becky Daum
Production Specialist: Dan Peluso

Photo Credits
AP Images: Terry Renna, 5; iStockphoto: serts, 31 (background); NASA, 10–11, 12–13, 14–15, JPL, 17, JPL-Caltech, cover (foreground), 20–21, 26–27, JPL-Caltech/Malin Space Science Systems, 8–9, JPL-Caltech/UA/Lockheed Martin, 22–23, JPL-Caltech/Univ. of Arizona, 6–7; Science Source: Detlev van Ravenswaay, 18–19; Shutterstock Images: albumkoretsky, 31 (parachute), Nattika, 30, 31 (egg), sandystifler, cover (background); SpaceX: 24–25

Design Elements: iStockphoto, Red Line Editorial, and Shutterstock Images

TABLE OF CONTENTS

CHAPTER 1

AN EXCITING
Landing

A spacecraft zoomed through space. It had traveled millions of miles. The trip took almost nine months. On August 6, 2012, it reached Mars.

Then it prepared to land a robot called a **rover**. The rover was named *Curiosity*.

Curiosity left Earth
November 26, 2011.

GETTING TO MARS

People waited for good news about *Curiosity*. **NASA engineers** watched their computers.

Other objects had landed on Mars. But none were as big as *Curiosity*. It was the size of a car!

Landing the rover would be hard. Something might go wrong. It could crash!

Curiosity landed by parachute.

GOING DOWN

The spacecraft hit the Mars air.

A huge **parachute** opened.

The spacecraft neared the ground.

Curiosity landed in an area called Gale Crater.

Then **rockets** fired. They slowed the spacecraft. It hung in the air.

Next came the tricky part. The spacecraft stayed in the air. It lowered *Curiosity* on a huge rope. It set the rover down gently.

Curiosity was safe on the surface. Everyone at NASA cheered!

ROVER TOOLS

Curiosity has many cameras. Its tools test rocks and soil. The rover also records the weather.

CHAPTER 2

THE RED
Planet

Mars is a cold planet. Its surface is rocks and dust. Some areas look like dry rivers. There might have been life once. **Scientists** needed a closer look.

Mars is the fourth
planet from the sun.

REACHING MARS

Landing on Mars would not be easy. Rovers leave Earth on rockets. The rockets shake and rattle them.

In space, there are dangers. The trip to Mars is long and cold. Sometimes the sun gives off bursts of power. These can damage machines.

Giant rockets start Mars rovers on their journeys.

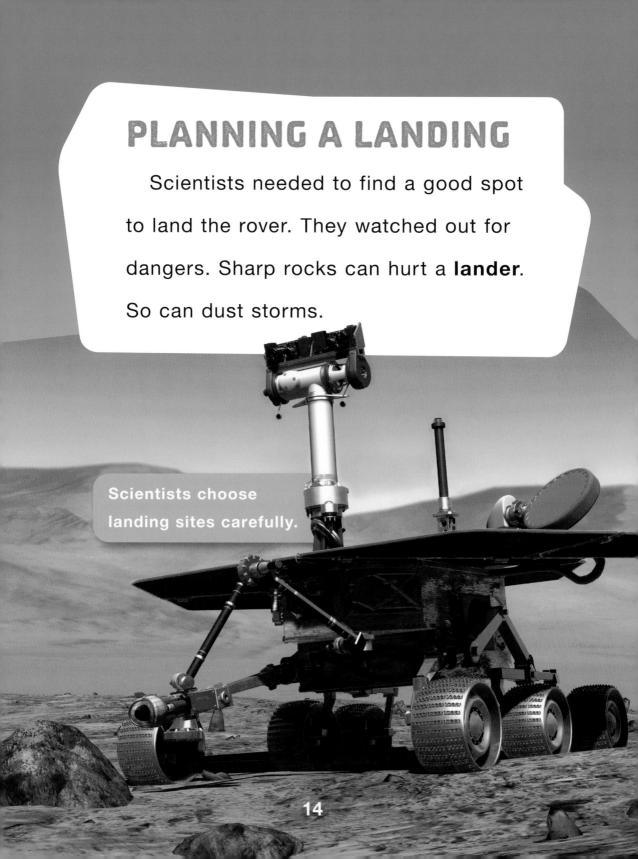

PLANNING A LANDING

Scientists needed to find a good spot to land the rover. They watched out for dangers. Sharp rocks can hurt a **lander**. So can dust storms.

Scientists choose landing sites carefully.

RED MARS

Mars's red color comes from iron in its soil.

Spacecraft travel very fast toward Mars. The air on Mars is thin. It doesn't slow down a lander very well. Engineers studied how to land safely.

CHAPTER 3

MISSIONS TO
Mars

NASA's first success on Mars came in 1976. Two landers arrived. They were called *Viking 1* and *Viking 2*.

The landers used parachutes. Then they fired rockets. This slowed them down. They touched down on three legs.

Viking 1 worked on Mars for six years. *Viking 2* worked for four years. They sent data to Earth. But they couldn't move around.

Viking landers looked for signs of life on Mars.

Spirit's lander floated to the surface.

A NEW PATH ON MARS

In 1997, people made a new kind of lander. The Pathfinder **mission** sent the first Mars rover. The rover could move around on the surface.

Pathfinder had a parachute
and rockets. It also had air bags.
These gave it a soft landing.
The rover rolled off the lander.

Two other rovers landed in
2004. They were named *Spirit*
and *Opportunity*. Both used air
bags to land.

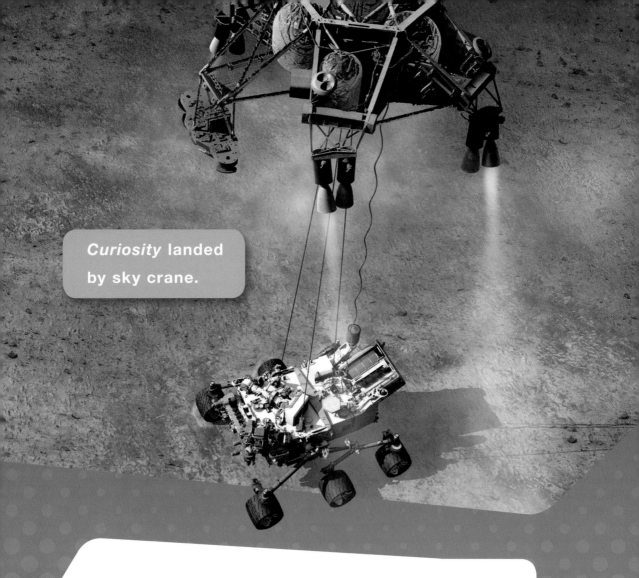

Curiosity landed by sky crane.

CURIOSITY LANDS

Curiosity brought new problems. It was much bigger than earlier rovers. Air bags wouldn't work.

Scientists needed to find a new way to land the rover. Helicopters gave them an idea. Helicopters hover. Then they drop cargo.

Scientists created a sky **crane**. This Mars spacecraft hovered. It lowered *Curiosity*. Then the spacecraft let go. *Curiosity* landed safely.

NEAR MISSES

The **Soviet Union** crashed two landers in 1971. One worked for just 20 seconds before breaking.

CHAPTER 4

MARS OF
Tomorrow

Landers help people study Mars.
Scientists learn about its weather, soil,
and rocks. One lander found ice. It saw
snow in the air!

The *Phoenix* Mars lander discovered snow falling on Mars.

PEOPLE ON MARS?

People have walked on the moon.
Someday people might walk on Mars.

A spacecraft will have to keep
astronauts safe. It must carry food
and air.

Scientists are planning new ways to land on Mars.

DANGERS ON MARS

Mars is dangerous. The planet is very cold. People can't breathe the air. People will need space suits to explore.

Engineers need to find new ways to land on Mars. *Curiosity* was big. Landers with astronauts will be even bigger.

Rovers never return to Earth. But astronauts will need a way to leave Mars. Engineers are working on these problems.

A CITY ON MARS

Someday people may do more than visit. They may stay on Mars. People would use water found on Mars. They would grow food in the soil.

For now, NASA will send more landers to Mars. Some old ones still work too. They still make discoveries. These help scientists plan future visits to Mars.

The *Mars 2020* rover will help scientists prepare for humans living on Mars.

GLOSSARY

astronaut
a person who goes to space

crane
a machine that lifts or lowers heavy objects

engineer
a person who plans and makes machines or buildings

lander
a spacecraft that lands on a planet or other space object such as a moon

mission
a trip into space for a purpose

NASA
the National Aeronautics and Space Administration, a U.S. government organization in charge of space-related science and technology

parachute
a large piece of cloth that fills with air to slow the fall of something tied to it

rocket
an engine that uses flames to move a spacecraft

rover
a robot that drives over the ground of a planet or other space object

scientist
a person who studies the world around us

Soviet Union
a former group of 15 republics that included Russia, Ukraine, and other nations in eastern Europe and northern Asia

TRIVIA

1. In 1966, the first human-made object landed on the moon. First, rockets slowed a ship. As the ship crashed, it threw the lander into the air. The lander then bounced on air bags.

2. Venus is the second planet from the sun. In 1970, a lander touched down on Venus. The thick air and a parachute helped slow the lander. Landers don't last long on Venus. It is blazing hot! No landers have been sent to Venus since 1984.

3. The Rosetta mission reached a comet in 2014. A lander touched down. Its legs took the force of the fall. The legs of the lander should have dug in with screws. But the screws failed. The comet was too hard. The lander bounced to a stop instead. The Rosetta mission ended in 2016.

ACTIVITY

LANDING AN EGG

Ask an adult before doing this activity. Find an egg. This is your lander! If you hold out your hand and drop it, the egg will likely break. Try to drop it so it doesn't crack. Use balloons, paper, a box, or anything else you want. Try your idea with a small rock first.

Did it work? Why or why not? Could you try something different? How can you safely land your egg?

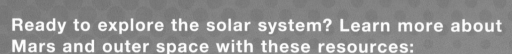

FURTHER RESOURCES

Ready to explore the solar system? Learn more about Mars and outer space with these resources:

Mars for Kids
https://mars.nasa.gov/participate/funzone/

Payment, Simone. *Mars*. New York: Rosen, 2017.

Solar System Exploration: Kids
https://solarsystem.nasa.gov/kids/do-it-yourself/

Want to become an astronaut someday? Suit up with these books:

Clay, Kathryn. *Astronaut in Training*. Mankato, MN: Capstone, 2017.

Lee, Pascal. *Mission: Mars*. New York: Scholastic, 2013.

Owen, Ruth. *Astronaut: Life as a Scientist and Engineer in Space*. New York: Ruby Tuesday Books, 2017.

INDEX